Making and Using Flash Cards

to accompany

Gerow
Psychology: An Introduction
Fifth Edition

prepared by

Josh R. Gerow
Indiana University--Purdue University at Fort Wayne

 LONGMAN

An Imprint of Addison Wesley Longman, Inc

New York • Reading, Massachusetts •Menlo Park, California • Harlow, England
Don Mills, Ontario • Sydney • Mexico City • Madrid • Amsterdam

Making and Using Flash Cards
to accompany *PSYCHOLOGY: AN INTRODUCTION, FIFTH EDITION*
by Josh Gerow

Copyright © 1997 Addison-Wesley Educational Publishers Inc.

ISBN: 0-673-97910-5

97 98 99 00 01 9 8 7 6 5 4 3 2

FLASH CARDS IN PSYCHOLOGY

As students, nearly all of us have had some experience using flatcars. For one purpose or another, most of us were first introduced to flash cards in elementary school. I can recall simple arithmetic flash cards that my second-grade teacher used. There was a simple problem on one side (8 + 3 =) and the answer (11) on the other side. Over and over, she drilled us on simple addition and subtraction problems. My other clear recollection of flash cards is of those I made for myself as I struggled with French vocabulary in high school. Do you have any memories of having used flash cards?

What I am proposing here is that this (very "low-tech") method can be useful in learning about many of the concepts and terms of general psychology. College students sometimes feel that flash cards are *too* elementary to be truly helpful. And, I agree that there *are* many learning situations for which flash cards may not be advisable. For learning basic vocabulary and for memorizing basic ideas and facts, however, flash cards have much to recommend them. In this booklet, I will do three things: (1) I'll explain why--or how--flash cards can be useful, (2) I'll provide some guidelines for making and using flash cards, and (3) I'll provide a **sample** of a few flash cards for each of the first five chapters of *Psychology: An Introduction, Fifth Edition*, just to get you started. I'm reluctant to provide too many, because the process of making flash cards can be as much of a learning experience as using them.

The Nature and Advantages of Flash cards

Let's first make sure that you know what I'm talking about when I talk about *flash cards*. These are cards -- and I see no reason to get any fancier than 3x5 inch index cards -- that are used to rehearse associative learning. Whenever you have two pieces of information -- say, a term and its definition -- and you are required to learn to *associate* one with the other, you will find flash cards useful. One piece of information (the term) is written on one side of the card and the associated information (the definition) is written on the other side.

Flash cards help you learn basic facts and vocabulary. It is important for you to realize that learning about psychology and preparing for exams involves more than just memorizing facts and the definitions of terms. Good exams will also test on conceptual understanding, relationships, the "big picture," and the application of facts. [This is why we ask "Before You Go On" questions and "Thinking Critically" questions throughout the text, and have provided booklets on critical thinking and "Practice Tests" in this package of materials for students.] What flatcars can do is help ensure that you know the basic foundations for the higher-level thinking that will be required on exams.

Flash cards have several advantages, most of which are quite self-evident.

1. They are portable. When carrying your textbook or your notebook is not convenient, you can always find a place for a few 3x5 index cards.

2. They help you practice *retrieval skills*; for example, exams require that you locate and retrieve information that you have stored in your memory. Yes, you do have to get that information *into* memory, which is what learning is all about. But on an exam, you will also have to get that information out of memory storage, which is what retrieval is all about. By using flash cards, you not only will be learning new information, you will be practicing retrieval, as well.

3. Flash cards help to inform you about what you know and where trouble spots may be.

Self-testing with flatcars can help you avoid surprises at exam time.

Making and Using Flash Cards

On the face of it, making useful flash cards should be a simple matter, and it is. There are, however, a few guidelines that you might want to keep in mind.

1. Place only one concept, term, or phrase on each card. Index cards are relatively inexpensive and it defeats the purpose of the cards to overload them.

2. At the same time, use only one card for each term, concept, or phrase. If you need more than one card to describe a concept or define a term, you're probably dealing with the sort of information for which flash cards are unsuitable.

3. You have to be careful with technical terminology but, whenever possible, use your own words. Remember, these cards are to help you, to provide *you* with cues for retrieving information from your own memory.

4. Be creative. Cards can easily accommodate simple drawings, pictures, diagrams, flow charts, and the like, just as easily as they can accommodate words.

5. Don't feel bound to the textbook. Flash cards can help you learn material from class as well as from the text.

6. Guard against "busy work." Attend to what you are doing and don't spend a lot of time simply copying information (particularly information you already know) directly from the textbook onto cards, just for the sake of making flash cards.

Procedures for using your flash cards are also reasonably self-evident. Again, however, there are a few guidelines I'd like you to keep in mind.

1. Once you have written a short pile of cards for a chapter, or for a Topic, shuffle them. Shuffle them again each time you go through the stack. You want to learn about the concepts of general psychology, no matter the order in which they appear.

2. Test yourself on both sides of each card. For example, for a vocabulary item, if you were to read the definition first, could you identify the term or concept being defined?

3. After you have gone through a pile of cards a few times, begin to sort them into shorter piles. You might start with two: "I know this for sure" and "I'm totally clueless." Obviously, a "I'm really not sure of these" pile can be useful, also. Once sorted into shorter piles, you'll know where you need to spend most of your flash card study time.

Please remember that the points I've listed here are *guidelines*, not hard-and-fast rules. Flash cards will help only if you make and use them. They are for you. Because there *is* benefit to be derived from creating flash cards as well from using them, I've provided only a sample of possible cards for the first five chapters of ***Psychology: An Introduction, Fifth Edition***. The rest is up to you. Good luck!

I here want to acknowledge the generous help of two of my colleagues at Indiana University -- Purdue University at Fort Wayne. Drs. Carol Lawton and Craig Hill helped to convince me of the value of a flash-card-approach to study, and provided most of the hints provided here.

SUBJECT MATTER
OF PSYCHOLOGY

RENE DESCARTES

SCIENCE

OPERATIONAL DEFINITION

behavior and mental processes

mental processes = affect (feelings, mood, emotion) + cognitions (thoughts, ideas)

philospher who explains humans without reference to God -- mind and body are separate but interact (interactive dualism)

1. organized body of knowledge
2. uses scientific method

defines a concept in terms of how the concept will be measured or created (e.g. intelligence = IQ)

TOPIC 1A	TOPIC 1A
WILHELM WUNDT	PHENOMENOLOGY

TOPIC 1B	TOPIC 1B
OBSERVER BIAS	SAMPLE

the study of events *as they are experienced*, more important than what they really are

a set or portion of a larger group (the population) chosen for study

Leipzig -- first psychology laboratory 1879 -- science of the mind/consciousness -- *structuralism*

when observer's (researcher's) own motives, expectations, and past experiences interfere with objectivity

TOPIC 1B

VALUE OF
CORRELATION COEFFICIENT

TOPIC 1B

VARIABLES IN
AN EXPERIMENT

TOPIC 1B

RANDOM
ASSIGNMENT

TOPIC 1B

DOUBLE-BLIND
TECHNIQUE

manipulate *independent variable*
measure *dependent variable*
control *extraneous variable*

+1.00 -- strongest *positive* relationship
0.00 -- no relationship
-1.00 -- strongest *negative* relationship

in which neither the participant
nor the person collecting the data
is aware of the hypothesis

making sure that each member
of a population has an equal chance
of being included in a sample

TOPIC 2A

PARTS OF
A NEURON

TOPIC 2A

RESTING POTENTIAL

TOPIC 2A

NEUROTRANSMITTERS

TOPIC 2A

COMPONENTS OF
THE A N S

the "tension" that develops
when the inside of a neuron is negatively charged (-70mv)
while the outside is positively charged

A N S = autonomic nervous system
= sympathetic and parasympathetic divisions

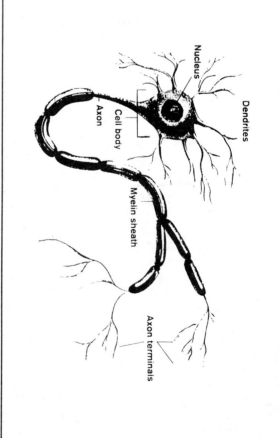

Dendrites
Nucleus
Cell body
Axon
Myelin sheath
Axon terminals

chemical molecules released from a
neuron's vesicles to either
excite or *inhibit* the transmission
of an impulse at the synapse

TOPIC 2A

ENDOCRINE SYSTEM

TOPIC 2A

SYNAPTIC CLEFT

TOPIC 2B

PARTS OF A
SPINAL REFLEX

TOPIC 2B

TWO MAIN FUNCTIONS
OF THE SPINAL CORD

system of glands that release hormones into the bloodstream (slower than nervous system)

at the synapse, the small space between the axon terminal of one neuron and dendrite of the next (where neurotransmitters go)

impulses go *in* on *sensory fibers*, *within* on *interneurons*, and *out* on *motor neurons*

1. spinal reflex behaviors
2. speed impulses to and from the brain

PARTS OF
THE LIMBIC SYSTEM

CORPUS CALLOSUM

PARTS OF
THE BRAIN STEM

LOBES OF
THE CEREBRAL CORTEX

1. amygdala (emotion)
2. septum (emotion)
3. hippocampus (memory)

1. the medulla
2. the pons

fibers that connect the left and right hemispheres
of the cerebral cortex --
severed in split-brain procedure

1. frontal
2. temporal
3. parietal
4. occipital

TOPIC 3A

A TRANSDUCER

TOPIC 3A

PSYCHOPHYSICS

TOPIC 3A

ABSOLUTE THRESHOLD

TOPIC 3A

RELATION OF LIGHT
TO VISION

study of the relationships between
the *physical* qualities of stimuli
and our *psychological* experience of them
(see Fechner, chapter 1)

1. wave amplitude -- brightness
2. wavelength -- hue (color)
3. wave purity -- saturation

something that changes energy
from one form to another
(such as our sense receptors)

the intensity of a stimulus that is just
barely detected -- more than 50% is *above*
threshold; less than 50% is *below* threshold

TOPIC 3A

RODS AND CONES

TOPIC 3A

NAMES OF THE SENSES

TOPIC 3A

PRIMARY HUES
PRIMARY COLORS

TOPIC 3B

STIMULUS FACTORS
IN PAYING ATTENTION

lights -- red, blue, and green

pigments -- red, yellow, and blue

transducers for light --
"photoreceptor" cells -- back layer of retina

contrast (in size, intensity, motion, etc.)
and repetition

hearing-audition; taste-gustation;
smell-olfaction; skin senses-cutaneous; visual;
balance-vestibular; and body position-kinesthetic

FIGURE-GROUND RELATIONSHIP

MENTAL SET

MÜLLER-LYER ILLUSION

RETINAL DISPARITY

in any one sense, we perceive only one stimulus (the figure) against the ground (background) of others

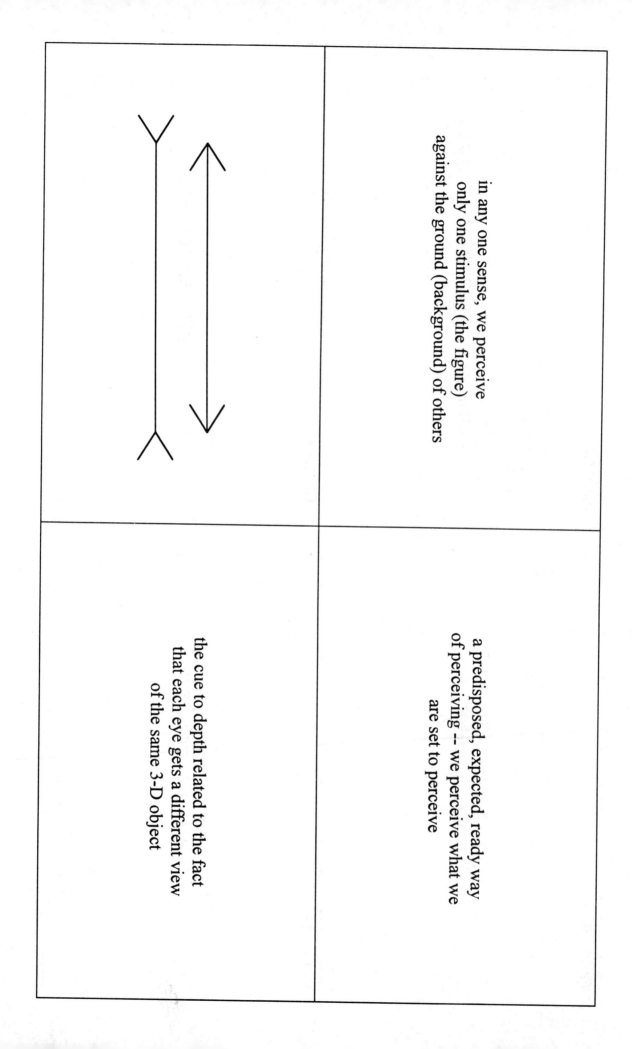

a predisposed, expected, ready way of perceiving -- we perceive what we are set to perceive

the cue to depth related to the fact that each eye gets a different view of the same 3-D object

FREUD'S LEVELS OF CONSCIOUSNESS

ELECTROMYOGRAM

JAMES'S CHARACTERISTICS
OF CONSCIOUSNESS

SUBLIMINAL PERCEPTION

consciousness (active awareness), preconsciousness (aware with effort), and unconsciousness (very difficult to become aware)

it is (1) changing, (2) personal, (3) continuous, and (4) selective perceiving, or reacting to, stimuli presented below one's absolute threshold

EMG -- a record of muscle activity used as an indicator of sleep

TOPIC 4A	TOPIC 4A
REM SLEEP	INSOMNIA

TOPIC 4B	TOPIC 4B
CHARACTERISTICS OF HYPNOSIS	PSYCHOACTIVE DRUGS

the inability to get to sleep or to sleep as much as one would like

chemicals which, in some way, affect psychological functioning

rapid eye movement sleep -- an indication of clear, vivid dreams

(1) increased suggestibility, (2) focus of attention, (3) exaggerated imagination, (4) not acting on one's own, and (5) acceptance of distortions of reality

TOPIC 4B

CHARACTERISTICS OF DRUG ABUSE

TOPIC 4B

EXAMPLES OF DEPRESSANTS

TOPIC 4B

EXAMPLES OF STIMULANTS

TOPIC 4B

EFFECTS OF MARIJUANA USE

caffeine, nicotine, cocaine,
"crack," amphetamines

a depressant, hallucinations, mood alteration,
reduction of nausea, lung disease,
memory impairment, chromosome abnormalities

(1) lack of control, (2) disruption of interpersonal relationship
and/or difficulty at work, (3) use more than one month

alcohol, opiates, heroin,
and barbituates

CLASSICAL CONDITIONING PARADIGM

GENERALIZATION IN
CLASSICAL CONDITIONING

LEARNING

ACQUISITION IN
CLASSICAL CONDITIONING

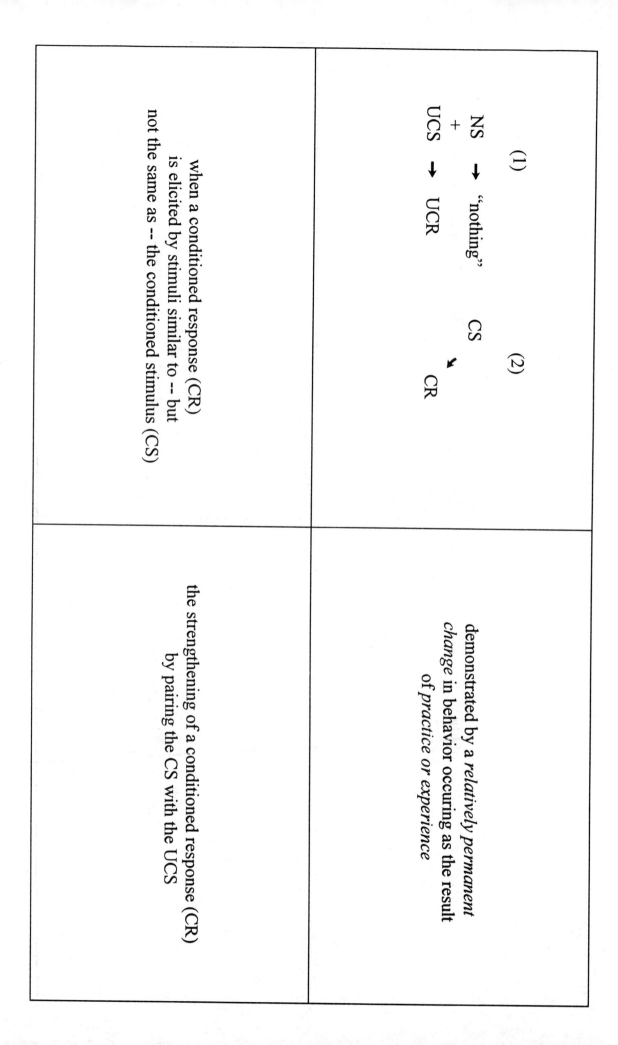

(1)

NS → "nothing"

UCS → UCR
+

(2)

CS → CR

demonstrated by a *relatively permament
change* in behavior occuring as the result
of *practice or experience*

when a conditioned response (CR)
is elicited by stimuli similar to -- but
not the same as -- the conditioned stimulus (CS)

the strengthening of a conditioned response (CR)
by pairing the CS with the UCS

TOPIC 5A	TOPIC 5A
PHOBIC DISORDER	TASTE AVERSION

TOPIC 5B	TOPIC 5B
LAW OF EFFECT	SHAPING

a classically conditioned response
of avoiding foods that have been
associated with unpleasantness, such as nausea

---

a disorder characterized by
an intense, irrational fear
(by classical conditioning?)

---

the processes of reinforcing successive
approximations of a desired response
until it occurs on its own

(Thorndike) responses that lead to
"satisfying states of affairs" tend to
be repeated or "stamped in"

SPONTANEOUS RECOVERY

NEGATIVE REINFORCER

PRIMARY REINFORCER

CONTINUOUS REINFORCEMENT SCHEDULE

a stimulus that increases the rate
of the response that precedes its removal

CRF -- the process of reinforcing each and every
occurrence of a desired response; opposite of an
intermittent schedule

the reappearance of a conditioned
response, following extinction and
a rest interval

one that does not need previous experience
to be effective -- tied to one's biology or survival (e.g food)